Are You REALLY His Good Thing?

ARE YOU REALLY HIS GOOD THING?

*Transforming Your Logical Yes
to a Spiritual Yes*

KYRIA M. WILLIAMS
AND CHRISSIE A. APPLEBY

XULON PRESS

Xulon Press
2301 Lucien Way #415
Maitland, FL 32751
407.339.4217
www.xulonpress.com

Scripture quotations taken from the Amplified Bible (AMP). Copyright © 1954, 1958, 1962, 1964, 1965, 1987 by The Lockman Foundation. Used by permission. All rights reserved.

Scripture quotations taken from the Holy Bible, New International Version (NIV). Copyright © 1973, 1978, 1984, 2011 by Biblica, Inc.™. Used by permission. All rights reserved.

Scripture quotations taken from the Holy Bible, New Living Translation (NLT). Copyright ©1996, 2004, 2007 by Tyndale House Foundation. Used by permission of Tyndale House Publishers, Inc.

Scripture quotations taken from the King James Version (KJV)–*public domain.*

Printed in the United States of America.

ISBN-13: 9781545657638

Table of Contents

Kyria M. Williams

Kyria M. Williams

If God tells her to, with no hesitation, Kyria is going to do it. Best known as an imminent marriage coach, Kyria M. Williams is a woman who puts no limitations on God. Kyria uses biblical principles to strengthen her own marriage and hope to aid other couples to do the same.

Kyria has been married to her husband LeConte (Trey) Williams for eleven years and counting and is a certified marriage coach through the Prepare and Enrich curriculum. Sitting under the leadership of Pastor Raymond D. Horry of Ark of Safety Christian Church for the past twelve years, Kyria learned the value of marriage and family. Her mission is to train and equip as many women as possible to help them understand how powerful the role of a wife truly is.

In 2014, Kyria joined Chrissie Appleby and the two worked as a team to launch a successful community marriage initiative titled, "I Married the Best Husband."

The concepts and skills that God has given Kyria to share with others are ones that have helped to strengthen her marriage and family.

In addition to serving as a marriage coach, Kyria is also founder of KMW Productions, LLC, a theatrical organization with a purpose to spread God's uncompromising truth. Kyria is proof that whatever God calls you to do can be accomplished with obedience, hard work, and persistence.

Kyria is now adding author to her name, *Are You Really His Good Thing?* is derived from her stage play titled, "Marriage Works, If, You Work It."

In Kyria's free time, she enjoys spending quality time with her prince charming husband and her two remarkable children, Sha'Kyra and Sharrod. To stay in the know, you may follow Kyria at www.kmwproductions.org and on social media @KMWPRODUCTIONSLLC.

Chrissie A. Appleby

Chrissie A. Appleby

If Chrissie could be described in one word it would be "Faith." God has given her a testimony to share with the world to prove "if He says it," you can be confident it will happen. Chrissie always believed in God, and she knew His hand was on her life, but it wasn't until 2011 when He became very real. Years prior, doctors told Chrissie it would be less likely for her to conceive a child. However, she heard the voice of the Lord say, "You and your husband will conceive a child." The Lord had her share what He had spoken publicly, so He could prove himself real to those who needed tangible proof. Four years later, she gave birth to a beautiful baby girl named Chelsie. The faith journey to conceive was only the beginning.

Chrissie believes the Lord has given her wisdom in the area of marriage through personal experience. Chrissie learned early on to seek guidance from the Holy Spirit daily on how to be a wife to her husband. In 2014, God gave Chrissie a vision to create an opportunity for wives to celebrate husbands called, "I Married the Best Husband" event. Chrissie and Kyria Williams co-founded and hosted the very first annual event in June 2014.

Currently, Chrissie is known for her God-given business SAFI. Chrissie followed the instruction of the Lord to make homemade lactation products to support breastfeeding moms. God placed it on her heart to provide doula services, and out of obedience, Chrissie became a certified prenatal, birth, and postpartum doula. Becoming a Doula triggered a passion to help with health disparities and mortality rates among minority women and babies due to birth complications.

God has added another title under Chrissie's belt, author. Chrissie has written a Children's book and now is the co-author of *Are You Really His Good Thing?* Chrissie loves going camping and spending time with her amazing husband, Shumari Appleby, and daughter, Chelsie. In addition, God blessed her with an extraordinary stepdaughter,

Shumara, and grandson, Kayden, who are her everything.

Whether it's sharing her testimony, lactation products, doula services, or books, she want God to always get the Glory and be a blessing to everyone she meets.

Acknowledgements

This work would not have been possible without my Lord and Savior Jesus Christ guiding and prompting me to write this book. I am especially indebted to Chrissie Appleby, the co-author who agreed to be a part of this project and worked actively to provide the time and attention to pursue this assignment.

I am grateful to each of the members of the KMW committee who has provided me extensive personal and professional guidance and taught me a great deal about team-work. I would especially like to thank my Pastor Raymond D. Horry, of Ark of Safety Christian Church. As my teacher and mentor, he has taught me more than I could ever give him credit for here. To my astonishing 1st Lady, Minister Kathy D. Horry, who has shown me by her example, what a good wife and life in general should be.

Nobody has been more important to me in the pursuit of this project than the members of my family. I would like to thank my mother & grandmother whose love and backing are with me in whatever I pursue. Most importantly, I wish to thank my devoted and supportive husband, Trey, and my two exceptional children, Sha'Kyra and Sharrod who provide unrelenting inspiration.

Kyria Williams

I want to thank my husband Shumari for being exactly what I needed in my life. You are the epitome of what a husbands love looks like towards his wife. I'm so grateful you chose me. I love you beyond my heart. Without you I couldn't have co-wrote this book. You have drawn me closer to God, caused me to seek God and to understand what it means to be "his good thang"

To our daughters Shumara and Chelsie, you both are my motivation. I strive to be the best example and role model to you. I don't take for granted the role God has given me in your lives. I thank you both for the love and support you unknowingly provide for me. To my grandson Kayden, you have given me so much joy and I love you dearly.

I want to thank my mom and stepdad for always supporting everything I do. Your love and guidance means the world to me. To my dad in heaven, he was my #1 hype man. He set the standard of how a man should treat a woman. I literally married a man like my dad.

To my Pastors Ken and Beverly Jenkins thank you for being our village, support, accountability, and friends. Because of your leadership you have given us the God-given tools to keep pushing when we wanted to give up.

Lastly, I want to thank Kyria for being obedient to the voice of God. You said that we would do something together and wow, a book. We thought it was the "I Married the Best Husband" Event. But you are such an amazing example of grace and a woman after God's heart and I'm honored to be a part of this book with you. You Rock Big Time.

Chrissie Appleby

Introduction of Book

*A*re You Really His Good Thing is a twelve-week analysis designed to inspire you to observe yourself and the way you play your role as a wife. If you didn't get an understanding of this role prior to your coming into the marriage institution, you have an obligation to study this and purpose in your heart to become all that God intended you to be.

If you desire to be a wife, these next twelve weeks will allow you an opportunity to prepare yourself and have a biblical understanding of what being a wife really entails.

The authors Kyria Williams and Chrissie Appleby both share an equivalent passion for marriage. So much so that they partnered and started the annual "I Married the Best Husband" event. The I.M.T.B.H. is an event where wives come together to celebrate, honor, and reverence their husbands just because. Kyria and Chrissie are unfaltering

1

about their biblical beliefs regarding God's teachings and hope through this book to expound on how much God values the institution of marriage.

We encourage you to read this book with your spiritual eyes. In order to receive the message and operate in the teachings of this book, you must first be a born-again believer, have the gift of the Holy Spirit, have an open mind, and have the heart to please God. If you don't, we pray that by the time you're done reading this book, it will have softened your heart and given you a hunger and a thirst to run after Jesus with your entire being. God is the only one that can transform our hearts to accept His teachings.

Some things will be familiar, some will be foreign, and maybe even disagreeable because of the culture we have been programmed in. However, it is not to condemn but to esteem, educate, and encourage wives and women desiring to be wives to understand, accept, and operate in our respective roles, so that we may please God and begin to see favor manifest in our lives as well as our husbands' lives. You have to be bold and unashamed to truly operate in obedience to God as well as in your role as a wife.

Let's jump right into the study and learn all about being a good thing "per God."

Chapter 1

CREATED FOR HIM

Section 1

Proverbs 18:22

*He who finds a (true) wife finds a **good** thing and obtains favor from the Lord.*

efore I start my day, every morning I spend some time alone with God in prayer and reading a few scriptures. On the morning of January 1, 2013, I came across the scripture referenced above. I'd always read that scripture with the assumption that a man who found a wife had apparently found a good thing. So, I asked myself a question...***"Am I really a good thing?"*** I was steered to dig deeper into the meaning of good. During the study, tears began to roll down my face because the answer to my question was clear; I was not operating in the characterization of being good. How could I not be a good thing when the Bible plainly says, "He who finds a wife finds a good thing?"

I'm ecstatic to share with you some of the things I learned during my study and to share God's Word and what it has to say about being a good thing.

One of the definitions for "good" is "having the qualities required for a particular role." Another one is "a benefit or an advantage to someone or something." So, ask yourself, "Do I have the qualities required for my role as a wife, and am I a benefit or an advantage to *(insert your husband's name)*?" Being an advantage to someone means that you put them in a favorable or in a more favorable position.

The complete scripture reads, *"He who findeth a wife findeth a good thing and obtains favor from the Lord."* Are you truly operating in your role as a wife, causing your husband to be placed in a favorable position? In order for us to exemplify being a good thing, we must **be a benefit or an advantage to our husbands**.

What I realized was that in order for me to be a benefit or advantage, I had to first renew my mind. I was drawing off of old information. Our minds store up memories and some things can constitute an impairment to our victory. Mind transformation happens on the inside, change of thinking is not the whole resolution; we have to go through a renewal. We are all raised a certain way, exposed to a certain environment, certain teaching, which invariably impacts the way we think. When transferring from our way of thinking to God's way, it's very challenging. We must be open and receptive to God's word, so that He can revamp our minds. I was stuck in my ways, stuck in my mindset, and stuck in the way I was doing things. Change is hard, and when we seek it, we certainly need the help of our Lord and Savior, Jesus Christ. We can't get there alone for apart from Him we can do nothing. We grow by going to a non-compromising, Bible-teaching church, spending time in God's Word, and adapting to His way of doing things. Doing things God's way always places us in a favorable position.

Section 2

Genesis 2:18

Now the Lord God said, "It is not good (sufficient, satisfactory) that the man should be alone; I will make him a helper (suitable, adapted, complementary) for him."

*I*n order to operate passionately in God's will, we must know and understand what scriptures and certain words within the scripture actually mean. Let's look at the word "helper. "It means "a person that gives assistance, support, etc". Once we have been chosen by our husbands, yep, that's right, you were chosen, our job is to now be of assistance and support to him. We should not come into his life and be a dominant, know-it-all kind of person; that is completely against God's will.

I'll use myself as an example. Before my husband and I got married, he'd been operating his own lawn care company for seven years. He was doing it all, the mowing, the estimating, the billing, the scheduling, etc. To him, he had a very successful company and was doing just fine. Then I came along with my extensive background in assisting executives; I thought I could just make changes immediately. I typed up letters and sent them out to all the customers explaining the new procedures. I changed the billing method and created a new scheduling sheet that he would use. I was so excited to do those things, thinking he would be so happy and grateful that those changes were going into effect. To me, in order to take his business to another level in professionalism, those changes needed to be made immediately. For the life of me, I couldn't understand why he was so upset. Why wasn't he jumping up and down in total excitement about my decision to implement those changes? I mean, why wouldn't I take matters into my own hands? After all, I was the one with the administrative background; I did that for a living, and I am his helpmate—right? With all my expertise in this area, the way I handled things was completely out of order and wrong.

How I went about doing things was far from being of assistance; I completely took over. Did I do that intentionally? Absolutely not! I didn't think then that I was taking over, I thought I was being a helpmate. That's why I stress the importance of understanding the meaning of words in scriptures. There are a couple more words in this particular verse that stand out to me, "suitable" and "adapted" for him. Suitable means "right for a particular person".

Adapted means "to become adjusted to new conditions". We, as women, are so used to being who we are. We have a "this is who I am" attitude. Either you like it or you don't. "I'm not changing who I am for anyone!" Well, if your overall purpose is to please God, then you are to become adjusted to new conditions. You and your husband are from two different backgrounds; you were raised one way, and he was raised another. You are two completely different human beings. But, the Word of God tells us that we are to adapt to him. What do I mean? You can't go into your marriage trying to change him.

Let me share a story. Before my husband and I got married, I used to laugh at the way he drove; it was a joke, and I'd often tell him that he drove like an old man, but it was so cute and funny to me. So, one day after we married, I was trailing him somewhere. He was driving so slow that it started to annoy me. Isn't that funny? The very thing that was so cute and funny before marriage, was tremendously annoying to me after marriage. Watch out; that's one of the enemy's tactics. Anyhow, as I was trailing him, I said out loud, "Oh my God, I cannot believe he is driving this slow!" As I put my blinker on and looked over my shoulder to make sure the coast was clear for me to get over because I was certainly going to pass him and make him follow me. The Holy Spirit stopped me in my tracks and said, "NO! You stay behind him and follow him, no matter how slow he goes." I heard the Holy Spirit, and I heard Him clear. Sometimes, we don't allow our husbands to lead because we think they're going too slow; they're doing it wrong; I can do it better. What I understand now is that God wants us to allow our husbands to lead; we are to follow them, even when we're not in agreement with how they're leading. We pray to God and trust that He will work all things out for our good.

Before you married him, you saw his way of living; you knew how much money he made and saw the car he drove. He probably even had to borrow twenty dollars from you to put some gas in his car, and all that. I'm joking, but if the shoe fits.... What I'm saying is when you married him, you accepted him and his way of life. Nagging him about getting a better job, driving too slow, wanting a bigger house, taking fancy trips, and comparing him to some girl and her husband on Instagram who you don't even know is not OK. If you're not comfortable with the way you guys are living, I recommend you to sit down with your husband, talk to him about your dreams and goals, and ask him what his are. Figure out how the both of you can work together as a team. You can encourage, cheer for, and assist him in going after the plans, but you can't get livid about a marriage that you voluntarily went into.

Hint for the singles... Make sure you have this discussion prior to marriage. Understand what his plans for his future are and make sure you're OK with following and assisting with those plans before you make a lifelong commitment.

Anyway, if I would've handled things differently and asked for my husband's approval, and whether he was OK with the changes or not, I would've accepted and been content with it. Just because we think it should be done this way or that way, does not mean he's going to be in agreement 100 percent of the time, and that is OK. The reason this statement can be a challenge to accept is that as women, we have an intangible quality, and that's wisdom. If you notice, in Proverbs, Solomon portrayed wisdom as a woman. In Proverbs 1:20-33 and Proverbs 8: 1-9, 12, wisdom is embodied as a woman who has much to offer—including "sustaining wealth and prosperity" and "life"—to anyone who would adhere to her words (Prov. 8:18,35). However, Solomon is not saying that women are essentially wiser than men, and he is also not saying that wisdom is a woman.

When we women truly tap into our value, it's powerful. Wisdom is you understanding that you and your husband will not always be in agreement with every decision made. Wisdom says that he's the man, and he's the ultimate decision maker. If you know in your heart of hearts that you're right about a situation, and your husband refuses to heed to your suggestion, pray to God about it, ask God to move on his heart and provide him (your husband) a clearer understanding of your suggestion. If it's God's will that it's done the way you suggested, allow him to make it happen and not you.

Wait, but my husband is not saved; he won't hear from God if God talks right in his face. We'll dig deeper into this in a later chapter. Now, don't go skipping all the rest of the chapters, to get to that one. Reading this book in its entirety will allow you to have a greater understanding and appreciation of the entire aspect of being a wife. If your husband decides to not go with your suggestion, follow him anyway (as long as it's not illegal, unethical, or against the express will of God), and allow God to get the glory out of your obedience. As my pastor often says, "It's not about who's right, but what's right," and what's right is always the Word of God.

Section 3

Matthew 19:4–6

He replied, "Have you never read that He who created them from the beginning MADE THEM MALE AND FEMALE, *and said, 'F*OR THIS REASON A MAN SHALL LEAVE HIS FATHER AND MOTHER AND SHALL BE JOINED INSEPARABLY TO HIS WIFE, AND THE TWO SHALL BECOME ONE FLESH*'? So they are no longer two, but one flesh. Therefore, what God has joined together, let no one separate.*

*W*ives, do you realize the significance of marriage in the sight of God? Do you understand that once you're married, you're no longer two, but one? You are so intertwined with your husband that God sees you as one. So, if you're the type of wife that bad mouths her husband before others, you are also referencing yourself. Whatever image you put out to others, as it relates to your husband, is also the very same image of yourself.. In Proverbs 31:12, it says, *"The wife comforts, encourages, and does her husband only good and not evil all the days of her life."*

It is our responsibility as wives to make sure we are operating in God's principles as it relates to the way we treat our husbands. Did you know that even when your husband is not in your presence, the above-referenced scripture can still be carried out? We can bring good to our husband's name when he's not around by the way we speak of him to others. We sometimes feel as if we need to vent, and that is quite fine, but we must make sure we're venting to the right person. It's OK to vent; the Bible even tells us that we can, but it says to vent to godly counsel.

Many times, we vent to the wrong people. We vent to the ones who are going to jump on our bandwagon and agree with everything we're saying. I have to go here, but often, we allow our emotions to get the best of us and find ourselves running to mama's house or that one girlfriend who's going through hell with her "boyfriend" but is quick to give her opinion.

Understand that once you guys make up and you forgive your husband, you guys are now back lovey-dovey. You have now placed him in a very uncomfortable situation by exposing some personal things about him to your circle. If you guys went through a rough season in your marriage and have now rekindled things, but he's still acting as if he doesn't want to come around your circle of friends or family, it's because you've destroyed his character. Your job is to now rebuild his trust. I pray that we recognize that venting to the wrong people is very detrimental in a marriage. Wives, it is EXTREMELY important that we have someone in our lives that can check us and help us understand when we are wrong.

Yes, sweetheart, sometimes you are wrong. And if I may be quite frank, most of the time, we are wrong. Wait, don't close the book, I prewarned you that you may disagree with some things in this book if you've never been exposed to God's uncompromising truth. However, when you begin to accept and operate in the truth of God's Word, you will begin to experience true freedom. Honestly, ladies, if we dive all the way into the biblical teachings of marriage and truly operate in our role as a wife, a huge percentage of our arguments will decrease. One of my favorite sayings is, marriage is God's gift to man; how we treat our marriage is our gift back to God. Let's be sure we're presenting our Father with the gift of excellence in our marriage.

After reading this chapter, I pray that you now understand what being a good thing and a true helpmate really means; accept its truth, and be the best you can be.

<u>Chapter 1: Created for Him:</u>
<u>Purposed to Action</u>

Questions

1. After reading section 1, can you honestly say you've been a good thing to your husband?
2. In section 2, we talked about being adapted for him. Think of something in your life that you do or say that your husband complains about often. Have you really examined that thing and actually put forth sincere effort to work on it, or is it going in one ear and out the other?
3. In section 3, we spoke of venting to wise counsel. Can you justly say that you seek wise counsel or that you vent to those who mean you no good when you are upset? I'm not saying some moms, sisters, friends, cousins, etc. don't give wise counsel, but if they don't, that's not who you should run to.

Purposed to Action

Choose one of the questions above and purpose in your heart to wholeheartedly put forth effort to work on that thing. Don't get down on yourself if you mess up, acknowledge it and try again the next time, but purpose in your heart to keep going.

Chapter 2
ROMANCE AND RICHES

Section 1

1 Corinthians 7:5

Do not deprive each other [of marital rights], except perhaps by mutual consent for a time, so that you may devote yourselves [unhindered] to prayer, but come together again so that Satan will not tempt you [to sin] because of your lack of self-control.

Why is it that when we are dating and fornicating, we are always willing and able, but the minute we transition into the institution of marriage and permitted to have as much sex as we want, all the aches suddenly begin? The headaches, backaches, stomachaches, eye aches, every ache imaginable. I remember some advice that one of my elder cousins said to me before I got married, she said, "Don't ever be too tired for your husband. Keep a box of Pepsi or an energy drink on the side of your bed. Drink it, and get busy." Her words were funny, and I don't think she meant them literally, but I got the picture. Remember in Chapter 1, I mentioned it is a must that we have someone to speak into our lives when we're off-track or not doing something correctly.

Let me share a story. Some years back, I found myself being so busy in life, I was stepping into purpose, and God was revealing the gifts He'd placed inside of me. I was counseling couples, writing plays, raising children, and working a job. How could I possibly have time to fulfill my duties as a wife as well, right "wrong"? I had to understand that out of every title I held, WIFE was the most important.

I repeat: WIFE is the most important. We oftentimes allow the title of MOTHER to overrule everything, even at the expense of our duties to our husbands. Being a mother is an essential responsibility, one of the most important responsibilities you will ever have, but again, it's important to not get so caught up in mothering that we lose focus of being a wife.

One morning during a counseling session, I was speaking with a wife who was always too busy in life such that by bedtime, she was worn out for the day. She never fathomed the idea of sex in her mind. So, the Holy Spirit began to pour into me words to speak to this wife about her situation. However, in the midst of the Holy Spirit ministering to this woman through me, He began to bring something to my attention. I had gotten so busy in life that being intimate with my husband was placed on the backburner. Later that evening, I received a call from someone who shared with me that God placed me on her heart, and she wanted to call to share what He showed her. She told me that God wanted her to tell me not to get so busy that I was neglecting intimacy with my husband. Wow, the same message, twice in one day. Everything was put on hold that day. I had to take a step back and realize I had become the woman I would minister to. Do you think it was hard for her to call and say that to me? Probably; but because I was open to correction and had asked God to use any willing vessel that He saw fit to speak into my life, I received her words lovingly and thanked her for being obedient.

But what I learned from that was that God is frank as it relates to sex within the institution of marriage. The Bible is very direct about sex. The Song of Solomon is an entire book dedicated to enjoying erotic love. God ordained sex and knows exactly what its purpose is. He gives clear instructions on how to use it and how not to. Within the precincts of marriage, sex is a beautiful thing. Can I offer a piece of advice to the wives? There's nothing wrong with wrapping your hair and putting your bonnet on, but please don't have it on while being intimate with your husband. Not even the ones with the rhinestones and all that. There's nothing sexy about a bonnet being on your head during intimacy. Take it off. And another thing, it is OK for women of God to wear sexy lingerie. Let's stop putting limits on our bedroom life, thinking it's offensive to God. The marriage bed is undefiled and what's offensive to Him is when we go against biblical guidelines concerning sex.

Come on wives; we're allowing worldly relationships to enjoy, more than we are, the very thing that God placed in the earth strictly for the institution that we're privileged to be in, namely, marriage. According to the Bible, sex between a married man and woman counts. Outside of marriage, it's an offense to God. Marriage is the only place to experience honorably the unwavering love that echoes our relationship with God. Do you notice that whenever we get upset at our husbands, we withhold sex from them as if our bodies belong to ourselves? The word of God tells us, "The wife does not have authority over her own body, but yields it to her husband" (1 Cor. 7:4). We'll talk more about this in the next section. Understand, ladies, that the act of sex between a husband and his wife is a reflection of our relationship with God. The enemy will play on your emotions and have you thinking that withholding sex from your husband will teach him a lesson. Wrong! The Bible plainly states that by withholding sex, we are placing them in a tempting state. The enemy has a target for sex in marriage, because it reminds him of God. If we truly understand what sex is intended to do, we'll have much more of it.

1 Corinthians 7:4

*The wife gives authority over her body
to her husband…*

uthority: "the power or right to give orders, make decisions and enforce obedience." A few synonyms for the word authority are power, control, charge, and rule. Ok, let's read this scripture, replacing the word authority with the actual meaning of the word. Here we go: The wife gives the power or right to give orders, make decisions, and enforce obedience over her body to her husband. WHOA! I literally just laughed out loud; I'm telling you, ladies, God is truly writing this book through me because I'm gaining knowledge right now, just as you are. Lord, have mercy…

Seriously, when we research words within the scripture and spell them out the way we did above, we are able to dig much deeper and get a completely better understanding of what the scripture actually means. The scripture we're referencing in this section is often confused with referring to sex only. Even though sex is one of the subject matters being implied, it is definitely not the only one. This scripture is also referring to attire, nutrition, exercise, careers, etc.

We have gotten so into this mentality of stating things like, "I'm a grown woman. I'm not his child. No man can tell me what to do. I'm going to do me, and I can care less who doesn't like it." With this way of thinking, maybe you really don't understand what being a wife consists of. Maybe you were so intrigued at the thought of being married that you didn't grasp what being a wife really entailed.

Before my husband and I were married, we went on a date. When he arrived at my house, I had on a really low-cut shirt. Back then, I was just going to church; I hadn't really developed an intimate relationship with Jesus. So, honey, I thought I was looking sexy as that thang. Anyway, immediately after he arrived, I opened the door. He came in, stood at the door, and I said, "Hold on, let me grab my purse." He then asked me one of the most humiliating, yet, at the same time, the dearest questions anyone has ever asked me: **"Where are you going with that shirt on?"** I thought he was joking, but he was so serious. He then said, "A virtuous woman doesn't dress like that. Please go change your shirt."

WHAT?

I remember that day like it was yesterday. I went upstairs to my room to look for a different shirt. While I was in my room, I was experiencing different emotions. As stated earlier, I was humiliated, so I started to allow worldly thoughts to enter my mind. *He's domineering, I don't know who he thinks he is. He just doesn't want anyone else to look at me. He got me messed up."* But while having all those thoughts, I also felt a sense of protection, which overruled those other thoughts. I eventually found another shirt and was happy to come back down those stairs and present myself as a virtuous woman, LOL. Even though he was not my husband at the time, I'm sure my reaction to his request gave me some brownie points. I do now carry his last name. Hey!

When you said yes to marriage, the place where God used to be in your life was now replaced with your husband. Of course, I'm not saying that you no longer have a relationship with God, but what I'm saying is in your single state, God is your head. But when you marry, your husband becomes your head. According to Ephesians 5: 22–24 it says:

> *Wives, be subject to your own hus-*
> *bands, as [a service] to the Lord· For*
> *the husband is head of the wife, as*

Christ is head of the church, Himself being the Savior of the body. But as the church is subject to Christ, ***so also wives should be subject to their husbands in everything [respecting both their position as protector and their responsibility to God as head of the house].*** See the umbrella below.

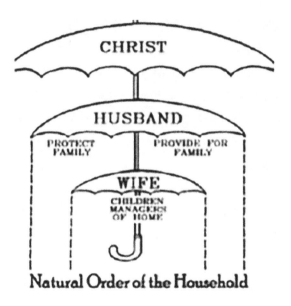

Natural Order of the Household

Understanding and operating in the above order will keep us under God's umbrella of pro-tection. The final thing I'm going to address in this section is trends. Ok, wives, hear me out. In the fashion world, we go through so many different trends with clothes, jewelry, makeup, shoes, etc., but what I want to address, as the Spirit directs, is this natural hair trend that has become extremely popular. I do understand if you like to keep up with all the fashion trends, and there's absolutely nothing wrong with that. However, if it is not pleasing in our husbands' eyes, we need to reconsider it. You see, wives, you may have girlfriends and even some family members who say things to you like, "Girl, please; if you like it, that's all that matters." However, 1 Corinthians 7:34 says, *"But a married woman is concerned about worldly things, how she may please her husband"*. So, those who are saying to you, "As long as you like it, that is all that matters," are not telling you the truth. It does matter what our husbands think about our appearance, and I pray that we, as wives, purpose in our hearts to allow our husbands to feel comfortable about being totally honest with us, without always getting so offended. I'm not knocking natural hair at all, because I am also natural. However, my husband doesn't care too much for some of the natural styles. He shared that with me after I tried one, and now whenever I'm trying a new hairstyle, I show him first to make sure he likes it. So, you see we came to a happy medium. I am still natural, but I allow him to approve my styles. Wow, "No she didn't say "allow." Yes, I did, sis, and I say it unapologetically. I know it's never easy to accept critiques, but when they're coming from valuable sources, such as our husbands, let's learn to receive the critiques in love.

Section 3

Proverbs 31:11

The heart of her husband trusts in her
{with secure confidence},
And he will have no lack of gain.

*T*he charge of managing our home should not be taken casually. As the scripture states above, our husband should be able to trust us with secure confidence. In some marriages, the husband manages the financial obligations in the household. And if that is the case, it is our job as wives to assist him with making sure that expenses of all kinds are kept under budget.

Of course, we always want to keep ourselves up and be attractive to our husbands. But let's not focus so much on the outward beauty and become wasteful of the family's hard-earned income on expensive clothes, jewelry, hair, lashes, nails, technology, and other things that are not a priority. I'm not saying we can't splurge on these things if our finances allow it. Prayerfully, we're not doing so at the expense of not paying tithes and offering, neglecting our homes as well as overlooking our inward beauty. Please, don't allow your social media image to take precedence over your husband's image of who you are.

Do you realize that outwardly you can have it all together—hair always done, nails freshly manicured with your beautiful gel polish and toes to match, your expensive clothes and purses, smelling of expensive fragrance, you have thousands of followers on social media, working your nine-to-five with a business on the side... I mean, you have it going on. But, sis, that's to your audience. What about the audience that really matters, your spouse and children? How do they see you? Are you so focused on those things that you are neglecting your obligations as a wife and mother? How can you walk around with all of that going on for yourself, and your husband can't stand the sight of you? Hear me and hear me well: with all of that you have going on for yourself, if managing your home and focusing just as much on your inward beauty are not your top priority, your husband can't enjoy all those things you put such an emphasis on because he's lacking gain.

First Peter 3:3-4 says: *"Don't be concerned about the outward beauty of fancy hairstyles, expensive jewelry, or beautiful clothes. You should clothe yourselves instead with the beauty that comes from within, the unfading beauty of a gentle and quiet spirit, which is so precious to God"*. I'm not saying that looking good and taking care of yourself is wrong; it absolutely is not. I would pray that we concentrate on both outer and inner beauty. Why not be the whole package?

How about your business on the side or what about you bringing more money to the table than your husband? Let's talk about that. Do you make your husband feel less than or feel that you are more superior because your income outweighs his? I pray, if you are doing so, that after reading this book you recognize how detrimental that mindset is to a marriage. Mark chapter 10 verse 8 says that when we get married, we are no longer two but one flesh. This applies to all areas, including finances. If we are operating on a "this is mine," "that is yours" mentality, our house is divided, and a house divided cannot stand according to Mark 3:25. We must do away with the single approach, renew our minds, and accept and do things God's way. After all, He did ordain the institution of marriage. How dare we go away from its original design?

My pastor often makes a statement that the husband is a thermometer, but the wife is a thermostat. A thermometer *reflects* the temperature of the environment. It simply reacts to what's happening around it. A thermostat, on the other hand, *regulates* the environment. The thermostat is always monitoring the environment, and if the temperature gets too hot or cold, it decides what to do to correct the situation. My prayer is that we will get back to God's original design for marriage, and we will gladly walk in our assignment as a thermostat.

If you don't know how to manage your finances or understand what's priority and what is not, seek out someone who is willing to sit down with you and show you how. Go to your local library or do a Google search to find different books that will aid you in this area. Don't make excuses as to why you can't do something; learn how.

Chapter 2: Romance and Riches:
Purposed to Action

Questions

1. When's the last time you made sweet, intimate, passionate love to your husband, not just lying there rushing it to be over, but really participating and enjoying the moment? If you are dealing with health challenges, please don't let this question condemn you, God understands and prayerfully, your husband understands. If not, ask God to provide him with an understanding of your situation.

2. Have you made a drastic change in your life or even to yourself? Did you ask your husband's opinion about the change? What are you prepared to do in the event he is totally against the change?

3. Are you spending money that you don't have on things that are not a priority, taking away from your household? Is your outer appearance more beautiful than your inward beauty, if so, how do you plan to work on that? If you are operating in the "this is mine," "that is yours" mentality, find out why and address the concern so your household can stop being divided.

Purposed to Action

Choose one of the questions above and purpose in your heart to wholeheartedly put forth effort to work on that thing. Don't get down on yourself if you mess up; acknowledge it, and try again the next time, but purpose in your heart to keep going.

Chapter 3
THERE'S POWER IN SUBMISSION

Section 1

Ephesians 5:22

Wives, be subject to your own husbands, as {a service} to the Lord.

*T*he word "service" means "the action of helping or doing work for someone else". I don't know about you, but it gives me great satisfaction knowing that as a wife, by submitting to my husband, I am helping and doing work for my Lord and Savior, Jesus Christ. I honestly don't think that we realize the power we possess as wives. In Genesis 2-18 it says, "It is not good for man to be alone, I will create for him a helpmate." As stated earlier in this book, we were created to be of service for our husbands. I read an article once titled The 1955 Good House Wife's Guide. The article was addressed to wives on how the husband should be treated upon entering his home after a long day of work. There were quite a few things the article stated, some I agreed with, and others I did not agree with. I'll share a few.

<u>DISAGREE</u>

• Don't complain if he's late home for dinner or even if he stays out all night. Count this as minor compared to what he might have gone through that day.

Hold up, now. This is not biblical at all. Ladies, even in our quest to be a good wife, we must use wisdom. Nowhere in the Bible does it say to allow our husbands to stay out all night and don't say anything. The devil is a liar! The Bible tells us to be understanding; it doesn't tell us to be fools. Know the difference!

<u>AGREE</u>

• Prepare yourself. Take fifteen minutes to freshen up. If you wear makeup, touch it up, and make sure your hair is in place and be fresh looking.

  ❖ I know this may seem a little overwhelming, but bask in the fact that you are his queen and men are visual. He has probably worked all day around beautiful women who smell good with lips freshly glossed, etc. Don't allow his mind to wander and wish his wife would do the same. We make sure we are looking right and tight when we're hanging out with our girls, right? Our husband wants to feel special as well. Whether you're a stay at home wife or a working wife, just take a few seconds, sis, to glance in the mirror, freshen up your lip gloss, and make sure your hair is OK, so you are presentable to your king.

- Clear away the clutter. Make one last trip through the main part of the house just before your husband arrives. Gather up schoolbooks, toys, paper, etc.

   ❖ This one is certainly for stay-at-home wives. If your husband has been out working all day, please don't allow the king to enter an out of order, chaotic home. I know what you're thinking, *I work just as hard as he does, staying at home is more of a job than any job out there.* I agree with you wholeheartedly. But, as stay at home wives, we must prioritize our schedule just as if we were working outside of the home. Yes, things happen that are out of our control sometimes, and there's nothing we can do about it. But the other days, as

43

mentioned above, take a quick second to make sure you look presentable; do the same with your home.

❖ Women that work outside of the home, don't get it twisted. Just because you work outside of the home, doesn't mean you shouldn't make sure you keep the home together as well. Again, don't allow our outside titles to interfere with our role in our homes.

❖ When we have company over, we clean, sweep, mop, dust, and even go buy a new thing or two. We make sure that the house is polished just right. We make our guests very comfortable in our homes. My suggestion is that we don't put more prominence on making our visitors more comfortable than we do for our very own king.

❖ Don't misunderstand me, ladies. I'm not saying that our husbands can't help us out, because most certainly they should. We are both adults, and the upkeep of the home should certainly be done by all parties residing in the home, but even if he don't, make sure you do.

• Prepare the children. Take a few minutes to wash their hands and faces (if they are small), make sure his daughter's hair is in place, and if necessary, change their clothes.

❖ *Girl, please. What do you mean prepare the children?* I'm glad you asked. What I'm saying is, for example, if they just ate ravioli, make sure the sauce isn't all over their faces and hands. Children love their dads, and when they walk into the home or room, they want to run over and hug him. Just make sure their hands and faces are wiped off, so you can save some money on having to put that outfit he had on in the cleaners because he has ravioli sauce all over it. The same way you take a quick second to make sure you and the home are tidy, do the same for the children. Again, whether they're already home or are walking into the house from daycare, make sure his princes and princesses are presentable.

❖ Be happy to see him. Greet him with a warm smile and show sincerity in your desire to please him. Listen to him; don't greet him with complaints and problems.

❖ This one is just saying, SMILE. Sometimes we wear the pressure of our days on our face, and upon greeting him, the entire mood is changed. I'm not saying to be phony, and if something bothers you, not to mention it; just know when the best time to bring it up is.

❖ Your goal is to try to make sure your home is a place of peace, order, and tranquility where your husband can renew himself in body and spirit.

Due to the changes that have taken place over the years and how our households are now run, unfortunately, we as wives feel as if we are superior, and that's the treatment our husbands should provide us. WRONG! Remember, they were not created for us; we were created for them. Am I saying our husbands can't do those things? Absolutely not; but he doesn't have to. Guess what? You don't have to either. But imagine how peaceful your home will be to the king of your castle. Again, I want to repeat the last bullet point listed above; it is our goal to make sure our home is a place of peace, order, and tranquility where our husband can renew himself in body and spirit. Considering this is not the norm, doing these things may sound foreign, but it is pleasing in the sight of God. Remember, submitting to your husband is ultimately submitting to God.

Section 2

1 Corinthians 7: 34

The unmarried woman or the virgin is concerned about the matters of the Lord, how to be holy and set apart both in body and in spirit; but a married woman is concerned about worldly things, how she may please her husband.

*L*et's break down the scripture pertaining to this section. An unmarried woman's focus should be on the things of God and Him alone. Don't get spooky spiritual; that doesn't mean you can't do anything else. You can still go out and enjoy yourself and have a good time and still please God. Now, a married woman's focus should be on worldly matters, such as how to please their husbands. Why does it seem as if the two are mixed up? It seems that unmarried women are more concerned about worldly matters, how to please their men, and wives are concerned with the things of God only. It's funny how Victoria's Secret and the gyms are filled with the unmarried, and the church is filled with the married. As a married woman, yes, you should go to church, no doubt, but that's not where every single second of your free time should be spent.

Unmarried women, you are in the most precious stage of your life. You are married to Jesus right now. You are getting to know Him for yourself. You are learning His ways, how to be treated, what you like and don't like... You are learning who God has created you to be. I like a saying I heard before that says a woman's heart should be so deep in God that a man has to go through God to get to her. How powerful that is! If he had to go through God to get to you, that means he had to learn from God Himself before approaching you. How can we go from a loving God that provides for us, loves us, heals us, and is there every time we call upon Him, to a man that treats us the total opposite? I submit to you, if you settled for that, you didn't spend the necessary quality time with God in your single state because if you had, there's no way would you have settled for anything less. Be mindful of how you represent yourself as an unmarried woman, in your attire, your social media posts, your conversations, where you go, whom you hang around, etc. You are a representation of your Father, made in His image. Be sure to act like it.

Married women, yes, we are to live holy lives unto God, and we are also to live pleasing to our husbands. We must find out what it is he likes and cater to that as well. We're not going to like everything our husbands like, but we must learn to adapt to some of their likes. I am speaking from experience; my husband is very adventurous. I, on the other hand, am not at all. At one point in our marriage, I couldn't have cared less about how adventurous he was. I told him I'd never do those things, and he shouldn't want me to either (i.e., bungee jumping, zip lining, camping, and all that type of stuff I never had a desire to do). I was trying to get him to stop doing the things he loved to do because I didn't like to do them. Then, I got to the point where I said, "OK, listen. You can do those things, but I won't." We would go out and go on trips, and he'd be doing those things alone, and I'd stand back and watch. I thought he was enjoying himself to the fullest.

One day, I asked my husband if he enjoyed being married. I asked him to critique me as "his" wife, not "a" wife (a big difference). His response was that he loved being married to me. He stated he couldn't ask for a better wife. I was all smiles. Then he said, "But sometimes I am bored in our marriage." My ears perked up, "What do you mean by that?" I asked. He said, "I would like for you to be more adventurous." Now I could've reverted back to my old way of thinking, which was *I don't care how adventurous you want me to be; I'll never be that!* But I didn't. I heard him; I received him, and I told him I would try something with him. I told him to take it slow on me that I'd try things little by little. You should've seen the smile on his face.

What did I do? I let him know that pleasing him was important to me, even if it went against what I liked. So, guess what? We took a trip to the Bahamas, and guess what I did with him? I went on a jet ski. Yes, I did it. I was terrified and only rode with him for maybe not even ten minutes, but I did it, and that really made him happy. Marriage is an institution where we have to learn to compromise; we have to learn to be selfless. We're not going to always agree with our husbands, but at least hear him out and take his ideas, decisions, thoughts, etc. into consideration.

On another note, if our husband asks us to do anything illegal, unethical, or against the express will of God, we don't have to do those things—use wisdom.

1 Peter Chapter 3:1-2

Wives, in the same way submit yourselves to your own husbands so that, if any of them do not believe the word, they may be won over without words by the behavior of their wives, when they see the purity and reverence of your lives.

We now dive into the section discussing the following statement, **"My husband is not saved."** The above scripture explains how the unsaved husband may be won over by his wife's actions, not her words. *What exactly does that mean?* you may ask. It means that we are losing our husbands by trying to win him to Christ with words versus our actions. Are you frustrated with your husband, comparing him to men that you perceive to be godly, hammering him over the head with the Bible because he seems to be dragging his feet on saying yes to God? Let me let you in on a little secret, sis: that method doesn't work.

In an effort to win your husband to Christ, it must be done with love, God's kind of love. First Corinthians 13:4-7 says:

> *Love is patient, love is kind. It does not envy, it does not boast, it is not proud. It does not dishonor others, it is not self-seeking, it is not easily angered, it keeps no record of wrongs. Love does not delight in evil but rejoices with the truth. It always protects, always trusts, always hopes, always perseveres.*

I therefore encourage you to do a detailed study of the significance of each one of the attributes above that explain what love is. It is vital that we love our husbands to Christ and not try to lip them to Christ. We must learn how to effectively communicate with our husbands in a style which they will receive. Learning your husband's style of communicating is beneficial. Every man is not the same; however, one thing they all have in common is that they ALL want to be respected. Speaking to him as if he is a child will not be received very well. Many times we have a valid point and are right in what we're trying to communicate. Conversely, the way we communicate at times is where the challenge is.

If you are a woman of God and are married to an unsaved man, you are the one God can use to speak to him. Ask yourself whether you are allowing the Holy Spirit to truly live and have His being in you. You are on an assignment, sis. Don't compare your husband to a saved man; he's not there, and truth be told, just because a man is saved, doesn't mean he and his wife are problem free. You don't know what that marriage looks like behind closed doors. Whether you're married to a man of God or not, we all are on different assignments.

While we're talking about being on assignments as wives, this is a good place to talk about being a helpmate again. Do you remember that in chapter 1 we broke down the meaning of help? If your husband is struggling in any area in his life, your mission is to help him overcome it. Whatever his struggle is, be it alcohol, drugs, slothfulness, pornography, immaturity, eating habits, and so on, your job is to help him through it. Saved as well as unsaved, men all have some sort of addiction or habit they struggle to overcome. Their addictions and habits which probably make them lose being in God's perfect will are one of the very reasons you are placed in his life. Genesis 2:18 says, *"The*

Lord God said, "It is not good for the man to be alone. I will make a helper suitable for him". Some of the habits, I know, cause a great amount of frustration that can make you want to give up and throw in the towel. Hear me and hear me well; you cannot be a helper in your own strength. The Holy Spirit must be alive and in charge. Otherwise, you will not be successful at accomplishing the set-out task. I will encourage you, ladies, if you start noticing changes in his behavior moving toward freedom from the bondage that has held him for so long, celebrate his progression. For instance, if he smokes an entire pack of cigarettes in one day and you notice he's not smoking as many, that's something to celebrate. Stop waiting to physically see the battle won and rejoice and cheer on the way to deliverance. Again, this advice is not the norm; it is biblical and not so popular. Will it be difficult? Probably! Is it guaranteed to work? No, it's not. But to witness the transformation and spiritual growth in yourself is a beautiful thing.

Have hope for your husband; treat him in a loving way, and don't belittle him because he is yet to arrive. Most importantly, pray for him. Praying for your husband when you really want to curse him out is one of the most difficult tasks; however, one of the most gratifying. The saying, "prayer changes things," may sound cliché, but it really does change things when you do it with a sincere heart.

Live your life in a way that will draw him *to* God not *away* from God. Do you find your husband often making statements like, "And you're supposed to be a Christian?" Sometimes he may say that to you just because he knows it upsets you. There are also times you may need to take a step back and evaluate if there can possibly be some truth to what he's saying. "Am I doing anything that is not representing my Lord and Savior that is causing him to say this to me?" Be honest with yourself, and allow the Holy Spirit that lives on the inside of you to correct you. Oftentimes, we don't want to admit our own faults. Proverbs 21:2 even says, *"Every man's way is right in his own eyes, but the Lord weighs and examines the hearts of people and their motives"*.

When we realize we may have handled a situation wrong, we should be humble enough to sincerely apologize. We, at times, allow our emotions to get the best of us, and let our flesh control the way we handle things. Understand it's not an overnight process, that's why it is crucial to have the Holy Spirit residing in you. The overall goal is to win your husband to Christ. If he decides to walk away, let it be because that is his choice not because of your actions. Proverbs 21:9 says, *"It is better to live in a corner of the housetop {on the flat roof, exposed to all kinds of weather} than in a house shared with a nagging, quarrelsome, and faultfinding woman".* Wow. So, if your husband is always away from home and hanging out in some of the darkest places yet you have a nice, clean, cozy home, and you wonder why he'd rather hang out there instead of being home with his family, ask yourself whether you are possibly the wife that scripture is referencing. The great thing about this is that there's hope for you. Maybe you just didn't know. Now that you've read this chapter, you know. So, when you know better, you do better.

I'm not saying we should be a pushover, ladies, and I am not recommending the unmarried women to run out and go marry an unsaved man. God's best for your life is to wait on Him. Be about His business, and in due season He will reward you with one of His precious sons that have prepared themselves and waited on God for you. But even when you marry your mature, on fire man of God, he will also have some areas in his life where your assistance will be needed to assist in his growth. Being a wife is honorable and a privilege when you see it in the spiritual realm.

Now to you ladies who have already entered into the state of marriage, but you were clueless about God's Word prior to your marriage, these instructions are for you.

I know when dealing with an unsaved man, we may deal with a lot of different things. Please, use wisdom. If your husband commits adultery or physically abuses you, please use wisdom and free yourself. The Bible does say that God hates divorce, but there are a few grounds for it if you choose to go that route. When adultery is committed, you have a choice to either stay in the marriage or get out; whichever way you choose to go, God will honor it. However, if you choose to stay, let's discuss some dos and don'ts. Do know that when adultery is committed, it's extremely difficult to get past. Do understand that forgiveness and trust are two different things. You can forgive, but that doesn't automatically permit the trust to be restored. I highly encourage counseling going forward. In an effort to move on and to make the best out of your marriage, understanding the underlying problem is essential.

When you feel you are ready to discuss the adultery incident, I say go for it. If you don't think you can handle the hardcore feedback your husband may possibly share with you, it may be best not to touch on the subject until you are absolutely ready. Let's be straightforward: we will never really be ready to discuss adultery, but again, in order to move forward, discussing the hard and uncomfortable things needs to take place. I must stress again, as stated in an earlier chapter, allow him to be totally honest with you about what caused him to go outside of the marriage. I'm not saying for you to take fault for your husband's negligence, but I will say hear him out and ask yourself if there is any percentage that you could have possibly contributed. Ouch, I know we don't want to accept this truth or even hear it, but again, if we want to grow from this, we need to hear the hard truths and be willing to grow in the areas that require improvement.

Let's discuss some don'ts. Don't constantly throw it in his face. Yes, he did it, and it was 100 percent wrong. I agree with you; but if you decide to stay, you're saying I'm staying to work through this, and prayerfully, both parties learn from the incident and never have to revisit this. Don't go and commit adultery yourself. When we're hurt, the first thing we want to do is make him hurt the way we hurt. As a woman of God, that is a big no. Keep in mind, you're not only hurting your husband, you will also hurt God and yourself. When God is head of your life, and your ultimate goal is to please Him, you don't want to do anything that causes you to sin as well as defame your witness. Remember, the enemy is after your marriage, and he will do anything he possibly can to destroy it. This is the enemy's job. Let's make sure, as women of God, we are doing ours, praying and living a life that is pleasing to God.

Chapter 3: There's Power in Submission: Purposed to Action

Questions

1. Can you honestly say you provide a peaceful and cozy atmosphere for your husband? If not, what are some things you can do to offer him that?
2. Has your focus been on pleasing your husband lately? Think back to when you first got married, all the nice little things you used to do for him. Do small gestures this week, something you may have stopped doing that you know he really likes.
3. Are you married to an unsaved man or even a saved man that's not yet mature in his walk? Are you married to a mature man of God but it seems that you two just can't see eye-to-eye on some things? Go to prayer, sis. Tell God exactly how you feel. Cry out to Him; spend time in His Word. Allow the Holy Spirit to truly have His way in and through you.

Purposed to Action

Choose one of the questions above and purpose in your heart to wholeheartedly put forth effort to work on that thing. Don't get down on yourself if you mess up. Acknowledge it and try again the next time, but purpose in your heart to keep going.

Chapter 4
TAKING BACK YOUR THOUGHTS

Section 1

2 Corinthians 10:5

Casting down imaginations, and every high thing that exalteth itself against the knowledge of God, and bringing into captivity every thought to the obedience of Christ.

*I*n the previous chapters, you have been given great insight and wisdom. I'm pretty confident you are encouraged. But in the back of your mind, you're probably thinking, *What about me? How do I continue being this amazing wife, mother, homemaker, and supporter?* As women in general, we are naturally giving and nurturing. We most definitely put everything before ourselves. We pour everything we have into our loved ones, and at times, we feel empty and wonder, *Who is pouring into me?* It's in those moments that the enemy will begin to have you questioning every-thing and everybody, especially in marriage. The enemy's whole objective is to find an entrance into our minds in order to create images and thoughts that are contrary to God's thoughts. Here's an example of how it works. I want you to visualize a pink squirrel with yellow ears, green polka dots, red feet, with a crown on its head. Does that actually exist? No; but our minds instantly see it, and at that moment appears a real image of a squirrel. In marriage, the same concept applies.

I am a wife, mother, doula, an entrepreneur, and work a full-time job managing two departments. On most days, by the grace of God, I handle all of those hats well, but on occasion, it can be overwhelming. I have an amazing husband who is super supportive and will help out all of the time. But me being a wife, I feel like I got this, and he should be able to come home and relax. Shoot reading Proverbs 31, she did it without complaining, so why should I complain? If you are not ready for this next level of transparency, I suggest you close the book now. No, for real, don't close the book. I promise this will be a blessing and pure freedom.

For about a year, I was noticing EVERYTHING my husband wasn't doing or saying. This is not to give the enemy credit, but in real life, he truly came to devour our marriage. If he can get you off of your game as a wife, he knows he can get to your husband. Remember what happened after Eve had eaten the apple, whom did God go to?

He went to Adam first! Okay, back to the story. It seemed like the more I focused on ALL the things my husband wasn't doing, distractions started pouring into several areas in my life. For example, my phone number has been the same for over eighteen years. I remember one of my exes sent me a text just saying hello, and he was proud of everything I had accomplished. Harmless, right? I would go to the grocery store, and I promise, every time, unfailingly, a nice-looking man would give me a compliment. Harmless, right? In normal circumstances, those comments would be harmless, but in the midst of chaos, those words would seem more valuable than my husband's words. In those times, the mind would begin to have you thinking, *My husband didn't tell me he was proud of me. Why did my husband not think I was beautiful? Does he not appreciate me? Is he not my biggest cheerleader, and is he not proud of my accomplishments?* Absolutely he was and still is, but just like the example of imagining the squirrel, my mind created a picture of my husband that was not true.

I know I'm not the only wife who has experienced this, and trust me, that is a real feeling. It seemed like when I allowed those subtle seeds to get planted in my mind all "hell" literally broke loose.

The enemy will take that feeling and plant seeds in your mind that will grow into thoughts like you are doing everything by yourself; your husband doesn't care about your feelings, and he doesn't acknowledge all you do for the family. That is the beginning of how Satan creates the *What about me?* thoughts in your mind. But guess what, God knows, and He cares about you. So you can ask God, "What about me?" And He will answer. He has given us everything we need to combat those thoughts in scripture.

In Philippians 4:8 says, *"Finally, brothers, whatever is true, whatever is honorable, whatever is just, whatever is pure, whatever is lovely, what-ever is commendable, if there is any excellence, if there is anything worthy of praise, think about these things"*). Paul is telling us to shift our thinking to regain our peace. When you start feeling over-whelmed, shift your thinking to things that are praiseworthy.

Sometimes changing your thoughts to focus on what's praiseworthy means changing your circle. Oh! You must surround yourself with women who will truly walk this out with you. Ask yourself when you are in your "feelings," and you pick up the phone, who do you call? Does that person agree with everything you're saying? Does she feed your spirit with godly wisdom? Or do you feel even more separated from your spouse after the conversa-tion? People mean well when they love you, but as stated in an earlier chapter, seeking godly wisdom is mandatory in marriage. Surround yourself with women who uplift and speak positively into your marriage and hear your heart. These women don't just hear the words you are speaking but hear also the unspoken words that can only come from discernment. They hold you accountable, and call you out when you're wrong. That's God answering the question, "What about me?" He will always send someone to tell you about "you" with godly love.

Section 2

Proverbs 31:10-31

A wife of noble character who can find?

henever we hear Proverbs 31, we instantly think about this woman who was an amazing wife, a homemaker, and a businesswoman. We have been to women conferences, ministries, and so on, titled the "Proverbs 31 Woman." I have even been called a Proverbs 31 woman, and every time I've heard that, I cringed. Why? That's such a compliment, but I've never seen myself that way, and quite honestly, it just seemed unrealistic, like an unachievable title. She seemed so perfect in all her actions, and I am far from perfect. However, when asking God about this section of the book, He revealed to me a different perspective of the Proverbs 31 woman that completely changed my thoughts. She wasn't a perfect woman, but she was a woman who understood her purpose. Once you understand your purpose, it eliminates all unnecessary stress, worry, and anxiety, or the comparison of yourself to other wives.

Since this section is about taking back our thoughts, let's look at the word "character" in the first verse. It's the reason why God starts the chapter off with the question *"A wife of noble character who can find?"* **Character** is the **mental** and moral qualities distinctive to an individual. Other words include nature, disposition, temperament, temper, and **mentality**.

The Proverbs 31 woman understood that in order to be successful in her God-given role as a wife, her **mind** and heart had to stay on pleasing God. Once we get married, it's mind-boggling how our thinking shifts to pleasing our husband as the priority instead of pleasing God first. It's not intentional, but the world has taught us to do that. We have all heard things like, "If you don't please your husband, someone else will?" This is foolish thinking. With that mentality, you become overwhelmed trying to do everything in your power to please your husband. Once you have created this unachievable goal to please him, the next comment that comes out your mouth is, "You are just too hard to please." And that's because you haven't asked God what it looks like to please your husband in the first place. Feeling that you can't please him will cause you to get out of character.

Refer back to the definition of character. Being a wife is not a one-size-fits-all role. God is strategic. He knows you are exactly what's needed for your husband and vice versa. Even though the bible says in I Corinthians 7; 34 that as a married woman, our aim is to please our husband, know and understand that God created your husband. He knows exactly what he likes and dislikes. Allowing the Holy Spirit to have free reign in your life will ultimately cause you to please your husband, because you are 1st obeying God.

When your husband thinks about your character, does he see God? Are you slow to anger? Are you patient? What is your disposition in the time of conflict? Our character should be a reflection of God's character. To understand God's character read Galatians 5:22-23. When your husband sees you, he should see a reflection of God's love. It will be unrealistic to assume each day will be perfect or that we won't step out of character, but the goal is to not stay there if we mistakenly step out.

I told the true story about how I used to flip out on my husband. When people hear this, it's hard for them to believe because of my true character. But let me tell you, I used to go into a full rage. My husband does not argue, so if any of you are similar to me, the worst thing anyone can do is sit there quietly in the middle of an argument, especially my husband. I remember one day I got so mad; I started throwing stuff and broke some of my belongings. My husband just said so politely, "Maybe you need to go lie down," and he left the house, so I could cool down. Him leaving actually made it worse, not because I thought he wasn't coming back, but it made me sit there in my mess. The Holy Spirit said so calmly, "You are not reflecting me," and that made me feel horrible and convicted.

Thank God I have the husband I have because that situation could have gone a totally different way. As wives, we can't be at home flipping out all of the time and expect God to not check us. Remember, we are to please Him first. Scripture tells us it's okay and normal to be angry, but we can't allow that anger to cause us to sin (Eph. 4:26). I am so grateful that I do not respond in that way anymore by the grace of God. Now, I am not saying I don't get upset, but I have learned the importance of striving to live in godly character. The Proverbs 31 woman always remained humble and meek. Remember your character is a reflection of God. In order to control our thoughts that turn into action, ask yourself, *Am I being a wife of noble character?*

Section 3

Mark 1:35

Very early in the morning, while it was still dark, Jesus got up, left the house and went off to a solitary place, where he prayed.

*L*et's talk about self-care. For a long time, I thought I was okay. I never thought about the importance of self-care or how the lack of self-care affected every area of my life spiritually, mentally, physically, and/or emotionally. I've never been the type to know how to relax prior to becoming a wife and mother. I always stayed busy, my mind stayed going a hundred miles an hour, and I struggled with saying no to anyone. I was so out of tune with myself that I couldn't identify that I was burned out. Once I was married and became a mom, it started to affect me mentally. I found myself being anxious more often, irritable, and exhausted. My prayer life began to suffer, yet, I felt justified. I mean I was fulfilling my duties as a wife and a mother, right? And I was struggling to also fulfill my God-given vision of becoming a doula and entrepreneur. So, surely this wasn't going to impact me spiritually. So I thought. It wasn't until I had an anxiety attack, was later diagnosed with anxiety disorder, and started feeling disconnected that I knew something was wrong and needed to change. This was by far one of the hardest moments for me to make a decision to start taking time out to put myself first. The thought of me taking time out to only focus on myself felt selfish; however, in Mark 1:35 even Jesus understood the importance of being disconnected in order to reconnect with the Father.

The importance of self-care can prevent anxiety, the feeling of being disconnected, and stress. Burnout is the first sign that it's time to reconnect to God and self. I came across an article about caregivers and burnout. Wives, we are naturally caregivers and at times spread ourselves thin. Here's a list of signs of burnout:

- Anxiety, depression, and/or irritability
- Feeling tired even after resting
- Cutting back on leisure activities
- Increased feeling of resentment
- New or worsening health problems
- Difficulty concentrating
- Neglecting other responsibilities

None of the above sounds like what God intended for us to feel as wives. Philippians 4:6 says, "*Do not be anxious about anything, but in every situation, by prayer and petition, with thanksgiving, present your requests to God*".Everything leads back to including God in our day-to-day activities and asking for instructions. God made us to be helpmates, so who would know more about what we need than He? Who can prevent us from falling into burnout other than Him? Psalm 55:22 says, "*Cast your cares on the LORD and he will sustain you; he will never let the righteous be shaken*" He is saying, stop taking ownership of burdens. It's truly that simple. Once we do that, we can start taking care of ourselves. How can we be "his good thing" if we aren't taking care of ourselves?

So what does this look like? First and foremost, it's spending time with the Lord. That can be sitting quietly listening to worship music, reading the Word, reading a Christian book, or daily devotional. It can be going on a walk around the park or your neighborhood, buying yourself something, treating yourself to a movie, dinner, or lunch. What I love to do is going to the thrift stores. I am not much of a shopper, but I can spend hours there. I found it to be super relaxing. But my all-time favorite thing to do once I get the house settled is to indulge in holiday movies. I believe in healthy eating and vitamins. When I eat something healthy, it really changes my mood. Little self-care moments can really change your thoughts and mood. Looking in the mirror and telling yourself, *You are amazing; you are an excellent wife; you are super creative, and girl, you are gorgeous,* are excellent forms of self-care. Become your biggest cheerleader.

Lastly, there isn't anything wrong with counseling. For some reason, we think counseling is bad or we are embarrassed to say, "I am struggling." God encourages us to seek godly counsel and wisdom. Read Proverbs 4:6-7 and Proverbs 19:20-21. Surround yourself with other wives who are after God's heart who are real, transparent, and who will hold you accountable, yet provide wisdom with love and encouragement. Taking care of yourself is an act of obedience. Our bodies do not belong to us. When we neglect ourselves, we actually neglect God. We are here to be a living example of who He is. He honors marriages, and the world is watching. Being a wife is a God-given role. We must take care of ourselves, spiritually, physically, emotionally, and mentally to live in our true purpose to be "his good thing."

Chapter 4: Taking Back Your Thoughts: Purposed to Action

Questions

1. What have you allowed to enter into your mind that is contrary to what God says about yourself, your husband, and your marriage? What can you do to combat those thoughts?
2. In regards to your character, if someone asked you and your husband to describe your character, would your individual answers be the same?
3. Make a list of what self-care looks like to you? How will you incorporate those items into your life?

Purposed to Action

Choose one of the questions above and purpose in your heart to wholeheartedly put forth effort to work on that thing. Don't get down on yourself if you mess up, acknowledge it and try again the next time. However, purpose in your heart to keep going.